Power Cut

A comedy in one act
by Keith Edmund

© Keith Edmund 1991

Published by:
New Playwrights' Network
35 Sandringham Road
Macclesfield
Cheshire
SK10 1QB

ISBN 0 86319 320 X

Suggested Stage Layout

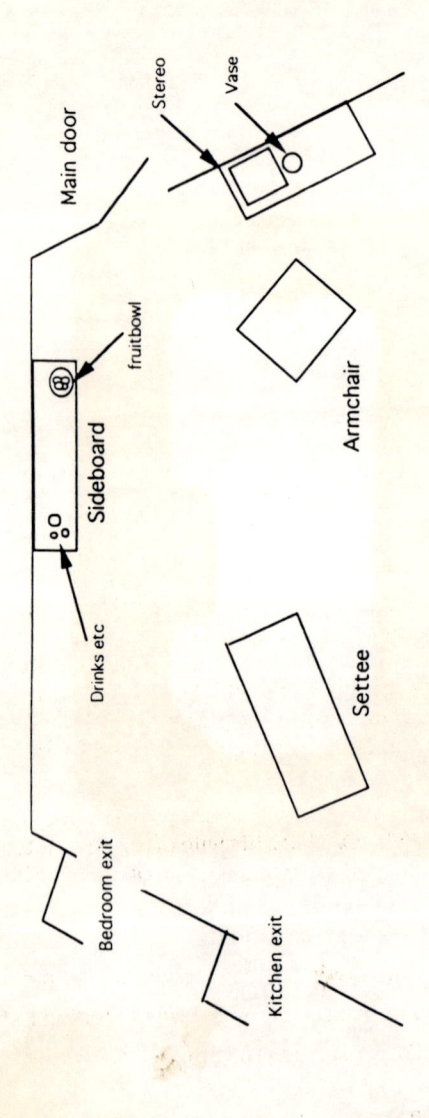

Power Cut

Characters:

David
Joanne
Martin
Sarah
Robert

Power Cut

Scene I

Time: Friday morning.

The main set, a living room in a modern apartment, is unlit as curtains open. The inset, stage left is a table laid with breakfast things. DAVID, a reasonably successful manager in his mid thirties, sits in the chair L. of table. He is dressed in a quality three piece suit and reads the Financial Times whilst noisily munching his cornflakes. He freezes occasionally, spoon held before open mouth, engrossed in what he reads. He takes occasional gulps of orange juice and coffee too, still barely taking his gaze from the newspaper.

The radio is playing Rachmaninoff's Rhapsody on a theme by Pagannini, (*or something similarly restful*). JOANNE, his wife of approximately the same age, enters sleepily stage L carrying a rack of toast. She wears an expensive night-gown.

            (JOANNE puts down toast and switches off radio)
DAVID   (*Not looking up; not too bothered*) I was listening to that.
JOANNE   Yes, well, it's all very nice I'm sure, but it's hardly Dire Straits, is it? (*She begins to butter the toast*)
DAVID   Dire what?

JOANNE	That stuff's enough to send you straight back to sleep.
DAVID	(*Not looking up; not really listening*) I'm not sure.....
JOANNE	What about ?
	(*She waits for response*)
	What aren't you sure about David?
DAVID	(*Looking up on mention of his name*) Mmm?
JOANNE	You're not really here, are you David?
DAVID	Eh?
JOANNE	The lights are on but nobody's home.
DAVID	Not with you.... sorry.
JOANNE	Never mind - go back to sleep.
	(*She passes him his toast, which he does not notice. A pause.*)
DAVID	(*Not looking up*) What are **you** doing today?
JOANNE	Mmm ? Oh...... I don't know. What's today anyway?
DAVID	(*Not looking up*) Thursday.
JOANNE	(*After a brief pause*) No, it's not. It's Friday.
DAVID	(*Not looking up*) Near as dammit.
JOANNE	(*Staring out vacantly*) Bedding plants.
DAVID	(*At last looking up*) Bedding plants?
JOANNE	Think I'll buy some bedding plants.
DAVID	(*Not at all interested*) Oh yes. (*He goes back to his reading*)
JOANNE	And some Iris bulbs. I want irises at the front this year.
DAVID	(*Not really listening*) Good idea.
JOANNE	Maybe a shrub or two......
DAVID	Did you say irises ?
JOANNE	......A small tree would be nice.
DAVID	Not irises for God's sake. I **hate** the bloody things! Remind me of funerals.
JOANNE	I like them.
DAVID	I hate them.
JOANNE	(*Loudly*) **I**....(*quieter*) ... like them - so we're having them.

Power Cut

DAVID	(*After a pause, going back to his reading*) Bloody ugly things.
JOANNE	You haven't forgotten tomorrow, have you ?
DAVID	How could I..... it comes after today.
JOANNE	You **have** forgotten.
DAVID	What - **what** ? What have I forgotten ?
JOANNE	Dinner - Martin and Sarah.
DAVID	Martin and Sarah ? You never said.
JOANNE	You've got a head like a sieve, David. I told you Monday.
DAVID	(*To himself mainly*) Martin and Sarah........ oh, no!
JOANNE	It's only one evening David, not the rest of your life.
DAVID	With Sarah's cooking, it could be both.
JOANNE	Well, what could I say? I've been putting them off for ages. She caught me on the hop - I couldn't think of an excuse.
DAVID	Anything would have done, Joanne. If you'd told her I had ballet classes I wouldn't have complained.
JOANNE	I'll use that one next time, David.
DAVID	He always calls me Dave. I **hate** being called Dave.
JOANNE	Then tell him for heaven's sake.
DAVID	Martin and Sarah on a Saturday night. Is nothing sacred ?
JOANNE	Planning to take me out were you?
DAVID	Well.... no.... not exactly.
JOANNE	Planning to slob it in front of the telly then.... by any twist of fate?
DAVID	Anything's better than an evening with those two. I tell you.... if they start arguing again I'm going. Last time it was just plain embarrassing.
JOANNE	Yes.... well....
DAVID	I've never known a couple so ill matched. If ever there was an advert for living in sin it's those two. I mean, if they're not arguing, it either means they've just had an argument or they're just about to have one. They even argue about who starts all the arguments.

Power Cut

JOANNE Oh stop moaning, David. I would have thought listening to them argue was a fair price to pay for flirting with Sarah.

DAVID Flirting with S - (*He makes to put down his cup on the table but misses, spilling its contents onto his crotch*)

Oh no! (*He stands quickly, surveying the damage*)

JOANNE (*Leaving L., hurriedly*) I'll get a cloth - don't panic.

DAVID I've got to meet a customer today! (*Shouting*) Why did you take my other suit to the cleaners? (*Looking back to the stain*) Oh my -

JOANNE (*Entering with a large, dripping cloth*) Is it **my** fault you've only got **two** suits? Scared to spend your money, that's your problem.

DAVID I've **got** to wear a suit today...... I mean..... I've **got** to.

(*Joanne is vigorously rubbing the offending area with the cloth*)

Careful! - I don't want pneumonia **there**!

JOANNE If it sneezes David, we'll give it a Beechams.

DAVID Get off.

(*He pushes her hand away and looks at the stain which, thanks to the wet cloth, is now twice it's original size*)

Jesus! - look what you've done!

JOANNE (*Calmly*) It'll dry.... don't make such a fuss.

DAVID Fuss? Would you buy a fifty thousand pound computer from a man with a damp crotch ?

JOANNE That would depend on how it affected his floppy.

DAVID Oh my God!

JOANNE Why don't you get the hair-drier on it?

DAVID Great idea, Joanne - I'll give myself a centre parting while I'm at it.

JOANNE That won't be easy with an 'Afro.'

DAVID (*Oblivious to her quip, looking at his watch*) Oh good grief... I've got to go. (*He knocks back the remains of his orange juice*)

JOANNE Why don't you put some tissues in there for a while?

DAVID (*Flustered, picking up his briefcase*) Tissues... yeah.... good idea.... I'll stick some tissues down there. Where are they ?

Power Cut

JOANNE   There's some on the side, out there. (*Indicating off*, L.)
DAVID   (*Pecking her automatically*) Right. See you later, then. Try and think up an excuse for tomorrow.
          (*He starts to leave*)
JOANNE   Oh David ?
DAVID   (*Stopping and turning*) Mmm?
JOANNE   Don't forget to take them out of the box, first! (*She laughs*)
DAVID   (*Completely straight-faced*) That's very funny Joanne. I expect I'll be laughing all the way to work.
          (*DAVID exits*)

JOANNE   (*Calling after him*) Unless you want to make a lot of new friends!
          (*She laughs again*)
          (*Taking up her coffee*) No sense of humour, some people.
          (*She smiles to herself, as lights fade to* BLACKOUT)

BREAKFAST INSET IS REMOVED IN BLACKOUT

          MARTIN and SARAH, a couple in their mid-thirties, are heard arguing as lights come up. They storm through main door up left.
MARTIN   (*Throwing jacket in armchair and going down centre*)
          Well if he flirts with you this time I'm going to bloody well say something! - I've had enough of it.
SARAH   Oh don't be so pathetic - he's only messing around.
MARTIN   Kiss kiss kiss..... the guy can't stop kissing.
SARAH   What **are** you on about ?
MARTIN   When he arrives.... when he goes.... he always has to kiss you.
SARAH   It's only on the cheek, Martin, he doesn't leap on top of me.
MARTIN   Who else do we know that's like that, eh.... answer me that?
          Family, that's all. You expect to kiss family..... you don't expect to kiss a guy you used to work with.

7

Power Cut

SARAH Nobody's asking you to, Martin.

MARTIN I mean, I don't kiss Joanne, do I ?

SARAH Feel free to Martin, if you feel hard done by.

MARTIN I don't want to. I've got no desire to kiss everybody that moves into my line of sight. A simple *hello* is sufficient. H*ello, nice to see you*, and... G*oodbye, are you sure you won't stay for another coffee*?' That's how most people act.

SARAH You're just paranoid.

MARTIN Did it ever occur to you that **I** might have made plans ?

SARAH Plans? You? Like renting a video and getting smashed on a bottle of cheap red wine ?

MARTIN Most wives would have said that they'll phone back to confirm.

SARAH (*Patronisingly*) **I** invited **them** Martin. Remember ?

MARTIN Suppose I'd booked a table at a restaurant, or something.

SARAH Martin, the last meal you took me out to was our wedding reception!

MARTIN Ha- bloody-ha.

SARAH You've got a nerve complaining about David flirting. What about you and Joanne ?

MARTIN Joanne ?

SARAH You're like putty in her hands.... (*Smiling wickedly*) ....and probably would be to, if she gave you the opportunity.

MARTIN What's that supposed to mean ?

SARAH Nothing, darling.

MARTIN It's just casual flirting, that's all. At least I don't salivate all over her.

(MARTIN *goes to sideboard and pours himself a drink*)

SARAH And if I'm cooking the meal, then you can damn well wash-up for a change. Go easy on that, it's all we've got.

MARTIN Are you starting on about that again? Honestly, it's like listening to the same record night after night.

SARAH You never wash-up.

Power Cut

MARTIN	Okay, okay.... I'll wash up! What's the big deal for God's sake? A bowlful only takes five minutes, tops.
SARAH	It's not how long it takes, Martin.... it's the sheer repetition of it. It's endless... it never stops.
MARTIN	Got a lot in common then, haven't you?
SARAH	I'm just asking you to help, Martin, just for once in your life. Ask me if there's anything you can do for instance...... I'm fed up of doing everything around here.
MARTIN	(*Sniffing*) Do I smell burning martyr by any chance?
SARAH	Tell me what you do, then..... apart from fixing the car.
MARTIN	I do plenty. Who does all the decorating, for a start?
SARAH	When did you last decorate?
MARTIN	It's not just that. It's a million and one things. Putting up shelves.... rewiring..... fixing things that go wrong.....
SARAH	Fixing them so they'll never work again?
MARTIN	Who creosoted the fence eh? Answer me that! Who -
	(*he struggles to think of something*)
	Who has to set the video when we go out, eh? Me! Because somebody else has got an irrational fear of knobs!
SARAH	We never **go out**, Martin. Why would I want to set the video?
MARTIN	What about mowing the lawn then? Who digs the garden eh? Who plants all the bloody vegetables?
SARAH	If you're referring to those six pathetic excuses for lettuces, I'd rather eat my bedding plants.
MARTIN	Oh I give up!
	(*He goes back to sideboard and tops up glass*)
	If that's all my efforts are worth, I don't know why I bother!
SARAH	I wasn't aware that you did. Are you going to drink all of that?
MARTIN	I'll have a damn good try.
SARAH	And I suppose because you don't have to drive tonight, you'll be marinating your liver as usual.
MARTIN	And <u>I</u> suppose you'll have two vodkas, giggle like a demented hyena all evening, and then want sex.

SARAH	(*Smiling insipidly*) Oh do let me put your mind at rest on that one, Martin. You won't be having sex tonight.
MARTIN	How do *you* know? You usually sleep through it anyway.
SARAH	It's all you ever think of, isn't it? Everything always comes down to sex.
MARTIN	I can dream, can't I? God.... if it wasn't for vodka I don't think you'd ever be in the mood!
SARAH	Women like a bit of romance, Martin...... something **you** wouldn't know anything about!
MARTIN	Saint Smirnoff - patron saint of bonking....
SARAH	(*Patronisingly*) You just don't get it, do you?
MARTIN	No. That's my complaint!
SARAH	Just try being a little loving.... a little thoughtful.....
MARTIN	(*Ignoring her*) Call me old fashioned, but I find the novelty of making love to someone who can barely stand up wears off quite quickly.
SARAH	I'm sorry Martin, I wasn't aware that standing up was a requirement!
MARTIN	You know what I mean.
SARAH	Well at least I'm willing to do **something** when I've had a drink. What do **you** do? Straight down the pub from work, then straight to sleep when you get in, apart from a brief period of consciousness while you burp your way through dinner!
MARTIN	It's not **that** often! I'm not the only bloke in the world that feels like murdering a pint after a hard day's work, you know.
SARAH	(*Going to kitchen door*) The difference is, with **you** it's **mass** murder!
	(*She exits. The doorbell is heard*)
MARTIN	(*Calling after her*) That line's too clever for you Sarah - where did you steal it?
	(MARTIN *goes to door and opens it.* ROBERT, *a neighbour, enters. He is roughly* MARTIN's *age, with a dry sense of humour. Clad for tennis, he carries a racket, a tennis ball and an audio cassette*)
	Oh hi Rob.... come in. You look exhausted...... Tough game?

Power Cut

ROBERT	It was, actually. Pretty damn tough. Someone's just wiped the floor with me.
MARTIN	Who's that?
ROBERT	Jenny in flat seven.
MARTIN	Jenny? But she's er........ only twelve, isn't she ?
ROBERT	Thirteen if you don't mind.
MARTIN	(*Amused*) Sorry.
ROBERT	She's a natural... great coordination. You'll see her at Wimbledon one day, you mark my words.
MARTIN	But Rob...... she's thirteen!
ROBERT	(*Not serious*) All right, don't rub it in. I'm depressed enough as it is. Anyway, can't stop, just dropped in to give you this. (He *holds up cassette*)
MARTIN	What is it ? Oh, that CD you told me about ?
ROBERT	Yup..... I've taped it for you. (He *hands it to* MARTIN)
MARTIN	Oh.... thanks. (*Pause*) Er... fancy a glass of wine ?
ROBERT	Er... yeah, okay. Yeah.... why not?
	(ROBERT *puts the racket on the sideboard and, after a moment's thought, puts the tennis ball with the apples etc. in the fruit bowl*)
MARTIN	(*Going back to cabinet and pouring drink for* ROBERT) You reckon this tape'll make a new man of me, eh ?
ROBERT	Doubt it.... but it'll give you a good laugh.
MARTIN	Not religious is it ?
ROBERT	No. Don't worry..... nobody's going to try and save your soul.
MARTIN	They'd be lucky. I haven't managed to save anything since I married Sarah, least of all, my soul.
	(MARTIN *hands* ROBERT *his wine*)
ROBERT	Thanks. No, it's just supposed to 'ease tension.... thereby enhancing the quality of close relationships...'
MARTIN	Really....?
ROBERT	That's what is says on the CD, anyway.(*Sipping wine*) This is nice.
MARTIN	Chateau Tight-arse, '92.

ROBERT	Excellent vintage.
MARTIN	(A *thought occurring*) We, er... didn't disturb you last night, did we?
ROBERT	Didn't disturb **me**, no. World war three wouldn't wake **me** up.
MARTIN	Thank heavens for that.
ROBERT	Put the fear of God into Gemma, though.
MARTIN	Oh no..... really ?
ROBERT	(*Matter-of-factly*) Sat bolt upright in bed at two a.m. and screamed, "Who the hell is that!"
MARTIN	Oh dear....
ROBERT	Well, actually she used an '18 certificate' word.... this is the 'PG' version.
MARTIN	What can I say, Rob? Please tell Gemma we're very sorry.
ROBERT	She was quite reasonable about it..... apart from telling me that if I didn't do something about it she'd staple me to the window box by my ears.
MARTIN	We were um.... both a little the worse for drink, I'm afraid. That's if you consider that Sarah could possibly be any worse.
ROBERT	Happens to the best of us. It's not your fault these apartments are made of cardboard.
MARTIN	I wouldn't mind so much if it was *good quality* cardboard. Anyway.... maybe this er..... tape will change all that.
ROBERT	You never know. There's a sound effect on there that's supposed to speed up hypnosis.
MARTIN	(*Sceptically*) Oh yeah!
ROBERT	S'posed to be a heartbeat I think. Gemma bought the thing at a junk shop. Thought it would help me with my smoking.
MARTIN	And did it ?
ROBERT	Not half. I went from ten a day to twenty a day. Still, I s'pose I should feel flattered, being remembered amidst all the arrangements.
MARTIN	Arrangements ?
ROBERT	For the wedding.....

Power Cut

MARTIN Oh! Right....... the wedding.

ROBERT Photographer, cake-decorators, printers, car hire.... the vicar. They all have to be told where they've been going wrong. 'specially the vicar. I tell you Martin, that guy's a couple of hymn books short of a full set, if you ask me.

MARTIN But it's.... all coming together is it?

ROBERT Slowly.

MARTIN I just hope you're as happy as....... (*thinking twice about the comparison*) .... well...... I er.... I hope you're happy.

ROBERT Gemma's on a strict diet, after my crack the other night.

MARTIN What was that?

ROBERT I asked if she'd told the photographer to bring a fish-eye lens so he could get all of her into one picture. It was only a joke, but she took it rather badly.

MARTIN (*Smiling*) Do you really want to get married?

ROBERT S'pose so. Can't stay happy all your life can you?

MARTIN I guess not.

ROBERT Anyway - must go. She'll be home soon.

MARTIN Well look, apologise to Gemma for me, would you. Tell her if there's any way I can make it up.....

ROBERT You have already, old chap.

MARTIN Have I?

ROBERT (*Handing empty glass to* MARTIN) Didn't I tell you? Best man's cried off - you're nominated.

MARTIN But I -

ROBERT Make the speech a good 'un! See you!

(ROBERT *exits quickly, grabbing his racket en route, but forgetting tennis ball.* MARTIN *is too stunned to complain about his appointment.* SARAH *storms in from kitchen, half of a broken long playing record in her hand*)

SARAH (*Holding record half up*) What's the hell's this?

MARTIN (*Embarrassed*) Ah......

SARAH When did you do this?

MARTIN Well, I -

Power Cut

SARAH	That was my record, you swine! I've just found it in the bin!
MARTIN	Sarah I -
SARAH	You've smashed it! You've smashed it to bits, you immature pig!
MARTIN	It was the other night, I -
SARAH	What gives you the right to smash someone else's property, eh?
MARTIN	If you remember rightly, Sarah, I -
SARAH	My favourite record! My favourite record, you swine!
MARTIN	(*Losing his patience, no longer embarrassed*) I was sick to death of the bloody thing!
SARAH	Oh were you ?
MARTIN	Yes I was... sick to death of it! It was driving me round the bend!
SARAH	You kid ! You big kid ! You and your stupid temper ! You destroy everything don't you? You make me sick !
MARTIN	It was the day you broke the roof-ariel on the garage door!
SARAH	That was an accident, damn you !
MARTIN	What if it was ? - It still snapped off !
SARAH	Your childishness never ceases to amaze me !
MARTIN	And your stupidity never ceases to amaze **me** !
SARAH	I hate you! You.... you.... you oversized kid !
MARTIN	And I hate you! You brainless moron !
	(SARAH *drops the record and stalks* MARTIN, *who backs away. She picks up a vase en-route - flowers still in it - and holds it aloft, ready to throw.*)
SARAH	You're going to be sorry Martin..... you'll never break something of mine again !
MARTIN	(A *little nervously*) Um..... your mother gave us that....
SARAH	(*Lowering vase, holding it with both hands*) That's true....
	(MARTIN *spots the tennis ball and takes it from the fruitbowl*)
MARTIN	Try this, it's softer....

Power Cut

(*He throws the ball to* SARAH, *who, in order to catch it, unthinkingly drops the vase. It smashes, and* SARAH *screams, unable to believe what she has done*)

SARAH (*Holding ball aloft, ready to throw*) You idiot !

MARTIN Calm down, Sarah....

(*Doorbell goes and* MARTIN, *who is right by it, opens it immediately*)

ROBERT (*Entering*) Did I leave my tennis ball here ?

(*He sees it and takes it quickly and calmly from* SARAH, *who is transfixed with the ball held aloft*)

Ah ! Thank-you Sarah!

(*He goes, immediately, leaving* SARAH *still frozen with one arm up in the air. She screams in utter frustration*)

MARTIN (*After a moment's pause*) Are you feeling a little tense, Sarah ?

(SARAH *does not answer, she just stares at him like a wild beast*)

MARTIN Only...... I've got a tape here....... a sort of hypnosis tape.

(*He hopes for a response, but* SARAH *just continues to glare*)

It's..... supposed to be quite good.....

(*Still no response*)

Sarah ?

(*Still nothing*)

I'll er........ put it on then...... shall I ?

...... yes........... I'll put it on.....

(MARTIN *goes to stereo, inserts cassette, but does not press 'play'*)

SARAH (*Relaxing her pose, through gritted teeth*) What is it, Martin ?

MARTIN It's just supposed to help you relax, that's all.

SARAH (*With venom*) I see.

MARTIN It's supposed to "ease tension"...... and er, and.... what was it ? Oh yeah..... "enhance the quality of close relationships." That's what it says on the sleeve of the record, anyway.

SARAH And at the end I suppose it says....... "you will go back to the shop..... you will buy all of my records"

MARTIN (*Monotone; straight-faced*) That's very clever, Sarah.

SARAH (*With venom*) I'm a very clever person, Martin.

Power Cut

MARTIN   Oh you are Sarah, you are.

SARAH   Put it on then.

MARTIN   What, **now** ?

SARAH   Yeah, come on, let's hear it.

MARTIN   Not exactly the ideal conditions, Sarah.

SARAH   We don't have 'ideal conditions' in this house Martin.

MARTIN   You'll just take the mick out of it, won't you ?

SARAH   Oh just play it for God's sake !

(MARTIN *considers this for a few seconds, then goes to stereo unit and presses 'play'*)

(*Sniffing the air*)   The oven!

(SARAH *exits hurriedly to kitchen*)

MARTIN   I don't believe it.

(*He presses 'stop', looks after her, awaiting her return, then changes his mind and presses the 'play' button again. The tape voice, which begins after a few seconds, is slow and measured, with a strong southern-states accent. As it begins,* MARTIN *crosses to armchair and sits on the arm*)

TAPE   Welcome. Welcome to intrafusion.

Intrafusion was born of theory, grew to be a concept, and now, for many Americans, Intrafusion is a way of life. It is the exploitation of your body's natural resources. It is the utilisation of the inner strength we all, as humans possess.

I will show you how to tap this hidden source of energy. I will be your guide.

Listen. Listen now to the heartbeat of the universe. The heartbeat will take you ever more swiftly towards..... Intrafusion.

(A *strange heartbeat-like sound is heard, which continues in the background for the remainder of the tape*)

The power we seek is not of the conscious mind, not of the sub-conscious mind.......... but of the *Anti-conscious* mind.

Intrafusion is the ultimate empathy; the only truth in a world of deception. To be *one* with the universe..... to be one with all life ....**that** is Intrafusion.

SARAH   (*Entering*) What a load of old codswallop !

Power Cut

MARTIN	Sshhh!
TAPE	With Intrafusion you can..... say goodbye to your tension..... ......say goodbye to your problems.....
SARAH	(*American accent*) ..... Say goodbye to your money.....
TAPE	To begin...... I want you to be completely relaxed....
MARTIN	(*Slightly tonelessly*) Sit down Sarah.... Listen to the heartbeat.
	(SARAH *goes to settee down R. She obviously finds the whole exercise rather tiresome*)
TAPE	Let your whole body relax ....
	Relax every muscle in your body............
	From the top of your head....... to the tip of your toes........
	Even your facial muscles........ let them relax.....
	(MARTIN *and* SARAH *do so*)
	Breathe slowly.... rythmically......... deeply..........
	Every muscle in your body is switching off...............
	Your body is inert, your mind is clear....... your breathing is slow,
	rythmic.... your muscles are all relaxed. You are one with life.........
	All you can hear.... is the sound of my voice........ I will guide you to
	Intrafusion........ I will open your mind.........
	You are completely relaxed..... totally relaxed.......
	MARTIN *slides slowly from the arm, into the armchair proper*)
	You are one with all living things....... you are life....... you are a part **of** life. You love all life..... you love every living thing.......
	You are part of the universe.... and the universe is part of you........
	(*After a pause*)

We are now going to return from our first exploratory trip towards the state of Intrafusion...... so that you can consciously assimilate this powerful new experience. On our next journey towards Intrafusion, we will travel to an even deeper level of the anti-conscious mind.

When I count to three, you will slowly return to your wakeful state. But you will remember what I have said...... and you will be filled with a new energy, a new desire to live life to the full. When you hear me say 'three', you will be completely awake....

One.... you are becoming aware once more of your surroundings.....

Two...... you can move freely, a new energy rising withiiiiiiiiiinnnn.

(Sudden and total BLACKOUT. Simultaneously the tape is heard to run down before the all-important number THREE is heard. After a few seconds, the lights come up again and the cassette is seen to pop right out of the stereo. MARTIN and SARAH gaze out with fixed, almost insane smiles on their faces.)

(Lights fade slowly to BLACKOUT)

END OF SCENE 1

Power Cut

SCENE 2

Saturday evening. MARTIN is pouring himself a drink. He moves, slightly slower than usual, down L, and sits in armchair. SARAH enters slowly from kitchen, reading a vegetarian cookery book. She sits on the arm of MARTIN's chair. They are dressed very casually - jeans etc. Throughout the following, regardless of anything that occurs, their dreamy smiles seldom leave their faces.

MARTIN	They'll be here soon, darling.
SARAH	Yes...... isn't it nice? I do look forward to seeing them again.
MARTIN	So do I. It's nice to have friends.
SARAH	You weren't so keen when I first told you.
MARTIN	No I wasn't. Strange, isn't it? I must have been in a bad mood or something.
SARAH	You said you don't like David kissing me when he arrives.
MARTIN	Now why should I feel like that I wonder? What a very silly and immature attitude for me to take. What's that you're reading, darling?
SARAH	(*Placing a hand on his shoulder*) It's the vegetarian cookbook **you** gave me, sweet-heart!
MARTIN	Do you.... do you like it now, darling?
SARAH	I love it! It was a wonderful thing for you to have bought me.
MARTIN	You threw it at me on our anniversary, I remember.
SARAH	I can't believe I'd do something so awful. It must have slipped out of my hand.

MARTIN	It slipped several feet across the room, as well.
SARAH	(*Hugging him*) Oh darling I'm sorry! That was the old me. I'd never do anything like that now!
MARTIN	(*Smiling*) I forgive you. After all..... if you can't forgive the girl you love...... who *can* you forgive?
SARAH	Oh Martin....... you're so romantic ! Shall we go upstairs again?
MARTIN	I don't think we've got time, darling. They'll be here soon.
SARAH	I suppose so. It's a shame we didn't say half past though, isn't it?
	(*They approach as if to kiss, but are interrupted by* DOOR BELL)
SARAH	Oh ! That's them...... I'll get it !
MARTIN	No, darling. You sit there.... I'll let them in.
SARAH	But dar-
	(MARTIN *puts a finger to her lips. He stands, takes her gently by the shoulders, and slides her back into armchair proper. Her legs dangle over the side*)
MARTIN	**I'm** the man of the house. At night, **I** answer the door.
SARAH	Oh, darling...... you're so masterful !
MARTIN	I'm your man. I'm here to love and protect you.
SARAH	And to dominate me !
MARTIN	(*Kissing her on the forehead*) Later, my princess.
	(*He goes towards front door*)
SARAH	(*Watching him*) What a gorgeous backside !
	(MARTIN *turns, blows her a kiss, then opens the front door*)
	(DAVID *and* JOANNE *are seen, both dressed very smartly.* DAVID *has a bottle of wine*)
MARTIN	Dave - Joanne ! Come in, come in !
	(*They enter*)
JOANNE	Hello Martin.
DAVID	And how are things with you ?
MARTIN	Wonderful, wonderful ! Here, let me take your coats !
DAVID	Where's the little lady ?

Power Cut

SARAH (*Leaping up from chair*) Here I am!
(*She goes to them*)
JOANNE Hello Sarah.
DAVID Hello there.
(*He pecks her on the cheek. As he withdraws, Sarah grabs him and kisses him fully on the lips*)
(*Joanne is surprised, but before she can think about it, Sarah hugs her forcefully*)
SARAH Joanne! It's so lovely to see you!
JOANNE Well it's er...... very nice to see you..... Sarah.
(*DAVID looks on, stunned, as MARTIN grabs his hand*)
MARTIN (*Shaking DAVID's hand, vigourously*) Oh Dave, it's so good to see you again, old friend!
DAVID Yes..... yes..... it's good to see *you* again, Martin. Um.... would you mind not calling me Da -
SARAH It's seems like ages since we last met!
DAVID Yes, well, two months **is** a long time, I suppose.
MARTIN (*Still shaking DAVID's hand*) Is that all it is Dave? Golly, it seems more like two **years**!
DAVID Yes, well..... can I have my hand back?
MARTIN (*Looking down, suddenly aware*) Oh! Yes.... sorry.... got a bit carried away! Come and have a drink.
DAVID Now, you're talking.
MARTIN Joanne. Vodka, Scotch, Martini?
JOANNE Oh...... um...... Scotch please. Scotch and American.
MARTIN (*Over-reacting; clapping a hand to his forehead*) Oh my God!
SARAH (*Concerned*) What is it darling?
MARTIN American! Joanne has American! I thought she had Dry Ginger - I've bought Dry Ginger!
JOANNE Dry Ginger's fine, really.
MARTIN But it's not your favourite, Joanne. I've let you down.
JOANNE No you haven't, don't be silly. I have either.... I don't mind which.

21

Power Cut

MARTIN   (*Lowering his hand, happy*) Really?

JOANNE   Really..... I'm easy.

DAVID   She wouldn't know the difference if you put mouthwash in, old mate.

JOANNE   (*Casting a disapproving glance at* DAVID) Just as long as it's fizzy, Martin.

MARTIN   Oh it's fizzy all right. Dave, how about you? Beer or a short?

DAVID   Oh... er lager, please.

MARTIN   (*Clapping a hand to his forehead again*) Oh my God!

SARAH   (*Concerned again*) What is it now, darling?

MARTIN   Lager! Dave has lager! I thought he had bitter - I've bought bitter!

DAVID   Bitter's okay.

MARTIN   But you'd prefer lager, wouldn't you Dave?

DAVID   Lager or bitter - whatever you've got. Not fussed.

MARTIN   (*Lowering his hand, happy*) Are you sure?

DAVID   Absolutely.

JOANNE   David wouldn't know the difference if you gave him cats -

DAVID   (*Quickly interrupting*) Thank you Joanne - we get the picture.

SARAH   So everything's all right, Martin. Joanne can have Dry Ginger and David can have bitter.

DAVID   (*Raising the bottle*) Oh yes, and stick this in the fridge for later.

MARTIN   Oh, Dave, you shouldn't have!

SARAH   Oh, David, Joanne..... how wonderful of you...... how thoughtful!

MARTIN   It takes **real** friends to make such a gesture!

DAVID   Steady on old boy, it's only a bottle of plonk!

MARTIN   (*With sincerity*) Well we appreciate it. (*He smiles, gormlessly*) I'll get your drinks.

SARAH   I'll help you darling.

(MARTIN *and* SARAH *exit to kitchen, looking back, smiling.* DAVID *and* JOANNE *look on in silence until the kitchen door swings shut. They turn to each other suddenly*)

Power Cut

DAVID	They're drunk !	)	> *Together*
JOANNE	They've had a row !	)	

DAVID	They've had a row ?	)	> *Together*
JOANNE	They're drunk ?	)	

DAVID	No I don't think so.	)	> *Together*
JOANNE	No I don't think so.	)	

DAVID   I've never seen anything like it in my life !

JOANNE   They're not drunk.... they argue **more** if they're drunk.

DAVID   Well they haven't had a row. They wouldn't bother hiding that - they never have before.

JOANNE   Well what then ?

DAVID   I don't know.... (*furtively glancing at kitchen door*) .... pot ?

JOANNE   Martin and Sarah ? Never !

DAVID   What if one of them had been prescribed something and they -

JOANNE   Valium !

DAVID   Sshhhhh!

JOANNE   (*Quieter*) Perhaps Sarah can't sleep.

DAVID   No. According to Martin, Sarah does altogether *too much* of that.

JOANNE   They're putting us on, they're putting us on !

MARTIN   (*Entering with tray of drinks*) Who's putting you on what ?

JOANNE   Oh.... er, they're er... putting us on flexi- time at work.

MARTIN   Are they ? Well that **is** good news. (*Handing her her drink*) But..... I didn't think you worked......

JOANNE   Ah ! Well, no.....but...

DAVID   (*Quickly interjecting, taking drink from tray*) It's where she **used** to work. They're bringing in flexi- time there.

JOANNE   Are they ? Oh yes.... yes of course they are !

MARTIN	Well it's a very good idea. Very civilised, flexi-time. Gives you a more relaxed outlook.... and I'm all for anything that does that.
DAVID	So am I...... absolutely!
MARTIN	I wish **we** had flexi-time. I could spend more time with Sarah.

(DAVID *starts to laugh but stops suddenly, when he realises* MARTIN *is serious*)

SARAH	(*Entering*) I hope nobody's desperate..... dinner will be at least half an hour, I'm afraid.
DAVID	Just as long as my glass is kept full, I can wait an hour!

(DAVID *takes a large mouthful of beer*)

SARAH	(*Smiling amiably*) You see, before you arrived, Martin delayed proceedings somewhat by screwing me on the breakfast bar.

(DAVID, *taken aback by this comment, discharges his mouthful of beer down* MARTIN's *front.* MARTIN *does not react at all to this; his smile remains intact.* DAVID *is highly embarrassed*)

DAVID	Oh my God!
JOANNE	David! How could you!
DAVID	(*Wiping* MARTIN's *shirt ineffectively*) Good heavens Martin, I'm sorry! What can I do? A cloth! Where's a cloth?
MARTIN	(*Calmly*) Don't worry about it Dave.... it's nothing.
SARAH	(*Smiling, also unaffected*) Go and change your shirt, darling.
MARTIN	(*Going to door up L*) Top Dave up, Sarah.
JOANNE	Jesus!
SARAH	(*Taking* DAVID's *glass*) No but seriously David.... he was like a wild animal.....
DAVID	R - really?
SARAH	There was no stopping him..... he was like a pneumatic drill.
JOANNE	Yes all right, Sarah....
SARAH	(*Hugging herself*) Thundering into me like a Saturn five rocket he was, David....

(*David stares, hanging on her every word*)

JOANNE	David isn't interested, Sarah.

Power Cut

SARAH	I never thought he'd stop.... getting me in all sorts of positions.....
JOANNE	Sarah please.... you're getting David all unnecessary....
SARAH	(*Softly*) All I know is, David......
DAVID	(*Entranced*) Y - yes ?
SARAH	Cornflakes will never be the same again.
	(*There is a hiatus*)
	(*Happily*) I'll get your drink.
	(SARAH *exits to kitchen.* DAVID *and* JOANNE *woodenly watch her go, then slowly turn to face each other. They remain still until* SARAH *returns a few seconds later with a can of beer. She hands it to* DAVID *who, staring vacantly at* SARAH, *puts it unopened to his mouth. He lowers it slowly, then* SARAH *reaches slowly over and pulls the ring pull. There is a small explosion of foam from the can and* DAVID *lets out a short gasp*)
	I like a man who drinks straight from the can.
JOANNE	(*Agitated*) He doesn't - do you David ?
DAVID	(*Vacantly staring at* SARAH) Mmmm ?
JOANNE	You prefer a glass, don't you, David ?
DAVID	That's right, Joanne.
JOANNE	David ! Wake up !
DAVID	(*Snapping back*) Ah ! What ? Oh yes.... sorry everyone. Went a bit blank there, for a moment.
JOANNE	Is anything the matter, Sarah ? With Martin I mean.....
SARAH	Martin ? No... why ? What's the matter with him ?
JOANNE	Well he...... well, he doesn't seem to be himself.
SARAH	(*Innocently*) Who *does* he seem to be ?
DAVID	What Joanne means is........ er..... what *do* you mean ?
JOANNE	Well I mean....... well, has Martin.....?
SARAH	(*All ears*) Yes ?
JOANNE	Er..... has he been, well...... ill lately ?
SARAH	Ill ? No..... no..... he hasn't been ill. Why do you ask ?
DAVID	Well he..... he looks a little run down, that's all.

25

SARAH	Does he ? Run down ?
JOANNE	Well..... maybe he's just a bit tired, or something.
SARAH	(*Smiling*) I'll tell him.
JOANNE	NO! (*composing herself after this automatic reaction*) No..... don't be silly. He looks fine, really.
DAVID	Yes, he looks great !
SARAH	He does ?
DAVID	Oh certainly.... great !
SARAH	Oh good. Another drink, Joanne ?
JOANNE	Er, no thanks - I haven't started this one yet.

(MARTIN *enters from kitchen, with* DAVID's *glass*)

MARTIN	Whose glass is this ?
JOANNE	(*Quickly*) It's David's.
DAVID	No it isn't...... I drink straight from the can.

(*He takes a swig*)

SARAH	Ah, Martin. Dave and Joanne were just saying how ill you looked.

(DAVID *nearly chokes on his beer*)

MARTIN	(*Not concerned*) Do I ?
JOANNE	No.... no, We didn't say that, exactly.
SARAH	Then they said you just looked run down.
MARTIN	I don't feel run down.
JOANNE	No.... tired ! We just thought you looked a little tired, that's all.
MARTIN	Do I ? Do I look tired ?
SARAH	No, it's all right.... because then Dave said you looked great!
MARTIN	Did he? (*He goes to* DAVID, *who has begun to cough again, and pats his back*)
	What a nice thing to say, Dave. I *feel* great, as a matter of fact. You're a lovely guy Dave, do you know that? A lovely guy.

(JOANNE *knocks back her drink in one go*)

Power Cut

JOANNE	I think I'll take that drink after all, Sarah.
MARTIN	(*Shaking his head*) A lovely guy.....
JOANNE	Straight Scotch this time.... if you don't mind.
SARAH	(*Taking Joanne's glass*) Coming right up.
	(SARAH *exits to kitchen.* MARTIN *waltzes around* DAVID *and* JOANNE, *smiling benignly*)
MARTIN	You know..... you're both lovely people.
DAVID	Well, s- so are y- you, a- and...
JOANNE	(*Nodding*) So are you and er....
DAVID	Sarah.
JOANNE	Sarah. So are you and.... Sarah.
MARTIN	Thank you !
	(MARTIN *waltzes over to stereo. Just as* DAVID *and* JOANNE *relax a little,* MARTIN *stops suddenly, becoming serious*)
	(*His back to them*) I love you. You know that, don't you ?
JOANNE	(*Transfixed*) M - me ? You love me ? Don't be silly.
MARTIN	(*After a pause*) No Joanne...... not **you**.
	(DAVID *is suitably worried, aware he is the only remaining choice*)
DAVID	I say.... you er... (*laughing nervously*) You er.... you don't mean....
MARTIN	(*Turning*) Both of you ! I love you both !
DAVID	Oh !)
JOANNE	Oh !) *Together, full of relief*
MARTIN	You're lovable people !
	(DAVID *and* JOANNE *laugh, embarrassed as well as relieved*)
JOANNE	Well....... so are you........ and.....
DAVID	Sarah ! You're nice as well !
JOANNE	Y- yes........ very nice.......
DAVID	You and Sarah.......
	(DAVID *and* JOANNE *nod emphatically*)
MARTIN	(*Pleased*) Well it's nice of you to say so.
DAVID	Not at all !

Power Cut

JOANNE	Think nothing of it !
MARTIN	(*Suddenly thoughtful*) But.........
	(DAVID *and* JOANNE *wait expectantly*)
	Do you........ **love** us ?
DAVID	**Love** you ? Steady on old chap..... I mean -
JOANNE	(*In a desperate moment of inspiration*) After all...... what **is** love ?
DAVID	(*Trying to pick up on this*) Y- yes. What is love ? How do you define it?
MARTIN	Well I love you...... that's how I define it. I love people........ I love all living things.
	(SARAH *enters*)
	But most of all.........(*turning to* SARAH) .....I love Sarah.
	(SARAH *goes to* MARTIN; *they cuddle*)
SARAH	And I love **you**, Martin !
MARTIN	I love **you**, Sarah....
SARAH	I love **you**, Martin.
MARTIN	I love **you**, Sar -
DAVID	(*Finally cracking*) Hold on - hold **on** ! What's this all about ?
MARTIN	What's *what* all about, Dave ?
DAVID	All this ! Are you two on something or something ?
SARAH	On something or something ?
DAVID	Are you two on drugs ?
MARTIN	Drugs? Who needs drugs, Dave? When you've got a girl like Sarah, you don't need drugs !
SARAH	(*Squeezing* MARTIN's *buttocks*) And when you've got a man like Martin, you don't need any other kind of stimulant !
DAVID	(*Exasperated, turning to* JOANNE) Do *you* know what this is all about ?
	(JOANNE *shakes her head*)
SARAH	(*Caringly*) You seem upset Dave. What's the matter ?
DAVID	What's the matter ? You two..... that's what's the matter !
JOANNE	David..... calm down.

DAVID	Look at them Joanne..... just look at them ! They haven't stopped smiling since we arrived.
SARAH	We're happy, David.
DAVID	I can see that. The question is, why? What happened to all the arguments ?
MARTIN	What arguments Dave ?
DAVID	What arguments - are you kidding ? You two fight like cat and dog!
MARTIN	Ah..... that's the *old* Martin you're thinking about Dave.
SARAH	(*Nodding*) And his wife...... the *old* Sarah.
DAVID	Oh really? And would you mind telling me where the *new* Martin and Sarah came from? Beamed in from another planet, were you? Or were there two giant seed pods by the side of the bed this morning?
SARAH	We've seen the error of our ways, David. We've found inner calm.
MARTIN	We've become one with the Universe, Dave.
DAVID	You've what ?
SARAH	We've journeyed into the anti-conscious mind.
DAVID	(*After staring with fixed smile for several seconds*) I'm going !
SARAH	(*Breaking from* MARTIN) David, please.....
DAVID	I don't know what all this is about, and quite frankly, I don't -
SARAH	You could come with us, David.
DAVID	Come with you ? Where ?
SARAH	To Intrafusion.
DAVID	Where the hell is Intrafusion ?
MARTIN	It's not a place, Dave...... it's a state of mind.
DAVID	Well your minds are certainly in a state, there's no denying that !
MARTIN	It's more than that, Dave. It's... (*imitating the tape*) ... *a way of life. It is the exploitation of your body's natural resources. It is the utilisation of the inner strength we all, as humans, possess.*
DAVID	This gets worse.

SARAH	(*Looking upwards and out*) Intrafusion is the ultimate empathy.
DAVID	Don't you mean the ultimate apathy ?
SARAH	(*Ignoring DAVID*) *The only truth in a world of deception. To be one with the universe....... to be one with all life..... that, is Intrafusion.*
DAVID	That's it - we're going. Obviously I'm excluded from the joke, whatever it is.
SARAH	It's no joke, Dave.
DAVID	It certainly isn't. Look... I'm sorry Sarah. I don't want to be rude but I've had a very hard day..... a very hard week, come to that. I'm just not in the mood for childish games.
JOANNE	David, calm down for goodness sake.
DAVID	No... I'm sorry.... it's too late for that. We're going home.
JOANNE	Oh, are **WE** ?
DAVID	Yes, we are.
JOANNE	No, we're not, David.
DAVID	Yes, we are. I've had enough of all this.
JOANNE	No.... **we're** not going, David.... **you** are.
DAVID	(*After a short pause to absorb this*) Oh I see..... it's like that, is it?
JOANNE	Yes.
DAVID	Well I hope you've got enough money for a cab, Joanne, because I'm taking the car.
JOANNE	That car is half mine, David.
DAVID	Well my half's going home.... what do you think about that?
JOANNE	You're not serious.
DAVID	I'm deadly serious Joanne. (*Feeling he has won*) Come on, let's go.
MARTIN	That's all right Dave. If it'll make you happy to go home then it's best that you go. I can take Joanne home in my car, later.
SARAH	Yes, Martin can take you home, Joanne.
JOANNE	Oh I couldn't put you to all that trouble, Martin.
MARTIN	Trouble ? It would be an honour and a privilege, Joanne.
JOANNE	Well, if you're sure...
DAVID	I don't believe I'm hearing this !

Power Cut

MARTIN	Of course I'm sure.
DAVID	Doesn't anyone care that I'm going ?
JOANNE	No David...... nobody gives a toss.
MARTIN	We want you to do whatever makes you happy Dave.
DAVID	STOP CALLING ME DAVE!
SARAH	If being away from us makes you happy, then it makes us happy as well.
JOANNE	I'll second that.
DAVID	This is your last chance Joanne.... I'm leaving!
JOANNE	Bye bye David.
	(DAVID *goes to door; turns*)
DAVID	You're all bonk raving starkers - I mean bark raving stonkers - I mean..... oh sod it..... you know what I mean!
	(DAVID *slams out. There is a momentary hiatus*)
JOANNE	Yes, well... I'm afraid I must apologise for David. He's never been one for jokes, especially when he's on the receiving end. His air-ioniser's on the fritz as well, which doesn't help.
SARAH	(*Confused*) Air-ioniser, Joanne ?
JOANNE	He's got one in the car, another in the office. He says the negative ions make him more alert.
MARTIN	I'm sorry to see him so unhappy.
SARAH	(*Nodding; concerned*) Yes....
JOANNE	He'll be back. He's been in a bad mood since yesterday.... lost an important sale.
SARAH	Oh dear..... I'm sorry to hear that.
JOANNE	Went to a meeting with his flies open and a wodge of tissues hanging out.
MARTIN	(*Innocently*) Why on earth did he do that ?
JOANNE	Ah... it's a long story. Anyway, you two.... what's it all about? Getting him back for some practical joke or something ?
	(MARTIN *and* SARHAH *are confused*)
	I mean, it's not that he doesn't deserve it but.... what's it all about?

31

Power Cut

SARAH	What's what all about, Joanne?
JOANNE	(*Laughing*) Come on, you can cut the act now.... he's gone.
SARAH	Cut the act?) *Together*
MARTIN	Cut the act?)
JOANNE	(*Serious*) It........ **is** an act........ isn't it?
MARTIN	I'm sorry, Joanne, I don't know what you mean.
JOANNE	All this stuff about Intrawhatsit...... all this smiling......
MARTIN	Intra**fusion.**
JOANNE	Whatever.
MARTIN	It's not an act, Joanne.
SARAH	Goodness, it's not **us** is it? Was it our fault that David lost all control?
JOANNE	Lost all control? You've got to be kidding!
SARAH	How do you mean, Joanne?
JOANNE	You want to see him lose control, come round at breakfast time. Watch him go berserk when his cornflakes go prematurely soggy.
SARAH	(*Going to* JOANNE) Oh my poor, poor Joanne. How you must suffer!
JOANNE	Steady on..... he's not an ogre!
SARAH	What other things make him go.... *berserk* then, Joanne?
JOANNE	I don't mean... I mean... *berserk's* a bit strong really. He says it's when his blood sugar level's low. He just gets grouchy, that's all.
SARAH	Well what sort of things make him grouchy then, Joanne?
JOANNE	Well... I don't know. That power cut in the middle of the film last night didn't exactly bring out his best side.
SARAH	Oh dear.... did you have a power cut last night?
JOANNE	Of course we did... the whole area was out for nearly an hour.
SARAH	You should have come round here.
JOANNE	What do you mean? You must have been affected too.
MARTIN	No....
SARAH	No, we weren't affected.

Power Cut

JOANNE	But they said on the local news. It was the sub-station or something..... the whole area was out.
MARTIN	Well, they must have made a mistake.
SARAH	(*Thinking*) We **didn't** have a power cut last night did we Martin ?
MARTIN	Of course not...... we'd remember that !
SARAH	(*Gazing off, vacantly*) It's just that....... (*she trails away*)
MARTIN	What ?
SARAH	(*Snapping back*) Nothing...... nothing. (*She smiles*)
MARTIN	(*After a short pause*) We'll play you the tape after dinner, Joanne.
JOANNE	Tape ?
MARTIN	The journey to Intrafusion.... it's on tape.
JOANNE	Wait a minute. Are you telling me it's for real ?
MARTIN	What's for real ?
JOANNE	You two...... being happy.
SARAH	(*Going to* MARTIN *and putting her arms around him*) Happy isn't the word, Joanne........ we're ecstatic.
MARTIN	It's shown us a side of ourselves we didn't know existed.
JOANNE	Really ? I think I ought to hear this tape.
MARTIN	And so you shall....... after the nut cutlets.
JOANNE	After the what ?
SARAH	Oh.... didn't we tell you ? We've gone vegetarian.
JOANNE	(*Not at all thrilled*) Oh....... how lovely.
SARAH	You see........ we love all living things, Joanne.
JOANNE	Except vegetables ?
SARAH	I'm sorry ?
JOANNE	Nothing. So anyway, how about hearing the tape **now** ?
MARTIN	Surely you'd rather wait until after dinner, wouldn't you ?
JOANNE	Well....... couldn't I hear a *bit* of it now ?
MARTIN	I suppose so....... if you don't mind delaying your nut cutlet.
JOANNE	(*Lightly sarcastic*) I think I can last a bit longer.

Power Cut

SARAH   Well, if it's what Joanne wants Martin, I think we should play it.

MARTIN   (*Beckoning her over to armchair near stereo*) Right, well.... come over here then, Joanne.

(JOANNE *obeys*)

Now if you sit here...... you'll hear much better.

JOANNE   But the speakers are over there.

MARTIN   (*Plugging in the headphones*) Ah yes..... but when I plug in these, the speakers are cut off.

JOANNE   Headphones ? I don't want to be unsociable.

MARTIN   You're not being unsociable. I just think it would be even better through headphones...... you won't have us to distract you.

(*He puts them on* JOANNE)

JOANNE   (*Loudly due to headphones*) Well if you're sure I'm not being rude!

MARTIN   (*Lifting phone from one ear briefly*) Far from it. You're being very open minded!

(*He goes to tape deck, inserts cassette and presses 'play'*)

(JOANNE smiles politely at SARAH)

MARTIN   (*After a few seconds*) Pity Dave left.

SARAH   Yes..... he could really benefit from Intrafusion.

MARTIN   Have you got a drink, darling ?

SARAH   Oh no...... I left it in the kitchen, on the breakfast bar.

MARTIN   Let me fetch it for you, darling.

(MARTIN *exits to kitchen*)

SARAH   (*Hugging herself dreamily*) The breakfast bar........

(MARTIN *enters with* SARAH's *drink and takes it to her*)

SARAH   You know it's funny isn't it ?

MARTIN   What's funny, darling ?

SARAH   That stuff about the power cut.....

MARTIN   Power cut ? Oh yes.... that. Peculiar.

Power Cut

SARAH   Joanne seemed quite adamant about it...... **so** sure in fact that..... (*she trails away*)

MARTIN   That what ?

SARAH   Nothing...... nothing.

(*They both look at* JOANNE)

How long will it take, darling....... the tape ?

MARTIN   You know, I don't really remember.

SARAH   I don't remember it being on for very long.

MARTIN   (*Confused*) I don't remember hearing the end..... do you ?

SARAH   No.

MARTIN   Do you think I should put it through the speakers ?

SARAH   No, it's too late now. Joanne would have to start all over again if you change it now.

MARTIN   Yes, you're right. I'll give it until dinner's ready, and if the tape hasn't finished then, I'll turn it off.

(JOANNE *is evidently being affected by what she is hearing and gazes out blankly.* DOORBELL *rings*)

SARAH   Now who could that be at this time of night ?

(MARTIN *puts down his drink and answers door. As he opens it,* DAVID *barges past him, filled with a new resolve*)

DAVID   Right, this is it. I want to know what all this is about, and I want to know right now. No double talk, no stupid grins, just a sensible explanation for why you two are acting like a couple of automatons.

(*He glares from one to the other, waiting*)

MARTIN   Automatons ?

DAVID   I should warn you, my blood sugar level's very low at the moment, and that doesn't put me in the best of moods.

MARTIN   Oh dear, would you like a nut- cutlet ?

DAVID   A nut- whatlet ?

SARAH   Are you about to go... *berserk*, David ?

DAVID   Eh ? What ?

SARAH   Joanne said that you sometimes go berserk.

Power Cut

DAVID	Oh did she? Well in that case, she's probably right. Yes... I think I **am** just about to go berserk.
SARAH	Oh dear.
DAVID	That is all right, is it? Or do I have to join your club first?
MARTIN	Club?
DAVID	Yes - the pre-frontal-lobotomy club, by the look of it.
MARTIN	We haven't got a club, Dave. We've just found enlightenment.
SARAH	Perhaps you need a few negative ions, David.
DAVID	Are you going to explain all this or not?
MARTIN	The best way to explain it to you is if you hear the tape.
DAVID	Tape?
MARTIN	(*Nodding*) The Intrafusion tape. You'll have to wait 'til Joanne's finished hearing it first, though.
DAVID	(*Spinning around to see* JOANNE) Oh my God! (*Going to* JOANNE *and taking her arm*) Right - that's it..... we're definitely going.
	(JOANNE *stands easily, but* DAVID *fails to notice her condition, and pulls her towards door.*)
SARAH	Let her hear the end, David.
DAVID	(*Still pulling, the headphone lead growing taut*) You two can believe what you like, just don't thrust it down other people's -
	(JOANNE *will go no further, the headphone lead preventing her.* DAVID *takes the headphones off her; she smiles, gormlessly*)
	It's no use arguing Joanne.
	(DAVID *unplugs headphones and thrusts them into* MARTIN's *chest. He drags* JOANNE - *still affected* - *out of door. The headphones thus disconnected, the tape voice comes once more from speakers*)
TAPE	**One**......... you are aware once more of your surroundings.
	Two........ you can move freely, a new energy rising within you.
	Three..... you are fully awake, a better person for your experience.
	(MARTIN *and* SARAH *snap back to their old selves*)
SARAH	What a load of old rubbish!

Power Cut

	(*Realising she is no longer on settee*) What the - ?
MARTIN	How did I ? (*Staring at* SARAH) When did you change your clothes?
SARAH	**My** clothes ? What about **yours** ?
MARTIN	(*Looking down*) Uh ? My God!
SARAH	Oh very funny Martin, very funny.
MARTIN	What ?
SARAH	How did you do that, you creep ?
MARTIN	What do you mean, how did I - ?
TAPE	On our next trip towards the state of Intrafusion we shall go even deeper into the anti-conscious mind........
SARAH	For God's sake turn that bloody rubbish off!
MARTIN	All right, all right woman!
	MARTIN *goes towards stereo. Before he reaches it there is another* POWER CUT, *just as the tape voice runs down:-*
TAPE	This time the energy will flow more freely, an energy that knows absolutely no limitaaaatttiiiiooooonnnnsss!!!!
MARTIN	(*In the darkness*) For heaven's sake..... **now** what ?
SARAH	That's all we need...... that's your fault Martin.
MARTIN	My fault ? For a bloody power-cut ?
SARAH	It's probably your rewiring - like I said, always fixing things so they never work again.
MARTIN	I suppose it's my fault if the whole street is out, is it ?
SARAH	Very probably.......

(*They continue arguing as curtains close and any remaining lights fade*)

* * * * * * * *

© 1991 Keith Edmund

FURNITURE AND PROPERTIES
Scene 1

Breakfast Area inset:

    Breakfast table & two chairs. Filled cereal bowl, two coffee cups, two glasses of orange, newspaper, radio.

Offstage: Rack of toast, wet cloth. (JOANNE)
Strike: After breakfast scene strike breakfast table, chairs etc.

Main Set:

    Settee, Armchair, Sideboard with drinks & wine glasses (L.H.S.) and fruitbowl (R.H.S.) Table/unit to house stereo equipment, breakable vase of flowers on unit (R.H.S), various cassettes, headphones with coiled lead.

Offstage: Tennis Racket, Ball, Audio Cassette (ROBERT)
Broken Long Playing record or CD (SARAH)

Strike: Broken Vase, used wine glasses.

Scene 2

Offstage: Vegetarian Cook book, Can of Beer (SARAH)
Bottle of Wine (DAVID)
Tray of Drinks, T-shirt, Beer glass (MARTIN)

LIGHTING PLOT
Scene One:

As curtains open, only breakfast area inset is lit.

Fade to blackout at close of breakfast scene, fade in on main set after inset has been struck.

Total blackout, simultaneous with run-down of Intrafusion sound effect. Three to five seconds later, fast fade in.

After five seconds of full lighting on the semi-hypnotized Martin and Sarah, slow fade to blackout.

Scene Two:

Total blackout for second power cut.
    (MARTIN - All right, all right woman!)

Power Cut

SOUND AND VISUAL EFFECTS PLOT

Scene One:

CUE 1   Opening music doubles as radio music and is 'turned off' by JOANNE.
(Suggested; Rachmaninoff's Rhapsody on a theme by Pagannini, Op. 43, Variation XVIII)

CUE 2   SARAH   "..... with you it's mass murder!"
                              DOORBELL RINGS

CUE 3   MARTIN   " I don't believe it."
                              Intrafusion tape, version I
                              (see production note 1)

CUE 4   AS LIGHTS COME UP FOLLOWING FIRST POWER CUT CASSETTE EJECTS FROM CASSETTE DECK*
(see production note 2)

Scene Two:

CUE 5   SARAH "It's a shame we didn't say half past though, isn't it?"
                              DOORBELL RINGS

CUE 6   MARTIN   "....if the tape hasn't finished then, I'll turn it off."
                              DOORBELL RINGS

CUE 7   DAVID   "It's no use arguing Joanne."
                              Intrafusion tape, version 2
                              (see production note 1

PRODUCTION NOTES

Note 1

The sound of the tape 'running down' is a useful mechanism for demonstrating that there has been a power cut. It may be produced in two ways;

1.) By using equipment which genuinely does run down in this manner when the power is cut.

2.) By recording the Intrafusion tape on a machine with variable speed. By INCREASING the tape speed during recording, the result will be the 'running down' sound on playback. If this second, more effective method is chosen, two versions of the Intrafusion tape will be required; the full length version, and also a second version of the last few lines of the tape with the run down sound effect coming later. (*See dialogue*)

If the tape 'run down' effect cannot be achieved it may be ommited.

Note 2

Ejection of the tape following the power cut is a useful mechanism for demonstrating that MARTIN and SARAH will not hear the remainder of the tape even though power has been restored. In the original production this was achieved by connecting a piece of thread to the EJECT button and looping it under the deck to a safe position in the wings. The effect was further improved by hooking an elastic band across the cassette deck opening prior to the cassette being loaded. In this way it was possible to eject the cassette right out of the player.

A simpler alternative would be to position the tape deck such that the eject button is obscured from the audience and can be operated by hand from the wings.